The Messy Monsters

Carousel Readers

Beverly Hoffman,
Jan Swartz, and Rebecca E. Shook

Illustrated by Kim Muslusky

DOMINIE PRESS

Pearson Learning Group

ISBN 1-5627-0382-X

Printed in Singapore
5 6   07 06 05

Dominie
Press
Pearson Learning Group

1-800-321-3106
www.pearsonlearning.com

Mom and Dad spent
all day Saturday
cleaning the house.

On Sunday morning, Mom went into the bathroom.

There were towels and dirty clothes
all over the floor.

The brush and comb were lying
on the counter.

There was water in the sink.

Someone had left the top off
the toothpaste.

"Oh my," said Mom.
"It must be those
Messy Monsters!"

Dad went into the bedroom.

The beds were not made.

Toys were everywhere.

Mountains of clothing
were piled in the corner.

"Oh dear," said Dad.
"It must be those
Messy Monsters!"

Mom and Dad went
into the family room.

The television was on.

There were comic books
scattered across the room.

Pillows were tossed on the floor.

Cereal was spilled on the table.

"Oh my," said Mom. "It must
be those Messy Monsters!"

Mom and Dad went
into the kitchen.

There was hot coffee
in the mugs.

There was hot buttered toast
on the plates.

"Surprise!" said those
Messy Monsters.
"We made breakfast for you."